I0088184

The Unified Theory of

Relationship Success

MARK LUEKER

The Unified Theory of
Relationship
Success

Copyright © 2020 Mark Lueker
All rights reserved.

Library of Congress Cataloging in Publication Data
Lueker, Mark
"The Unified Theory of Relationship Success"
Library of Congress Control Number: 2020902165

ISBN 978-1-7345933-0-3

This book is dedicated to my parents,

David and Darlene,

whose lifelong love defined the term
"successful relationship."

CONTENTS

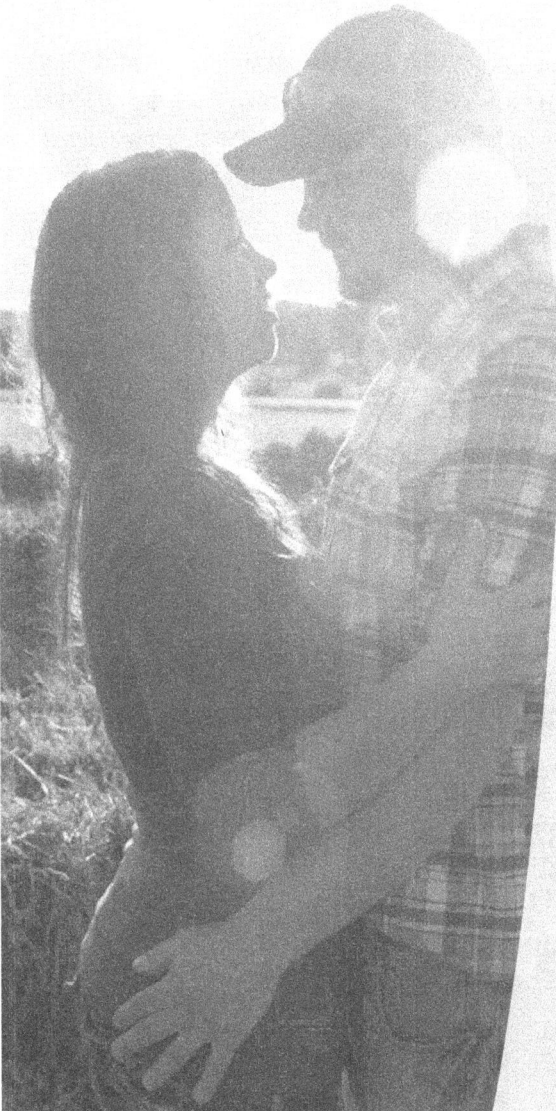

CHAPTER ONE

Introduction

Relationships are formed and dissolved every day throughout the world, what creates a successful relationship and why?

How can you learn to identify and then support a relationship that meets your own emotional, physical, spiritual and intellectual needs?

Many long-term relationships start out as expressions of joy and then degrade into two people who can't afford to get away from each other, or do not really enjoy being with each other, or are apathetic about their partner in the relationship, and many other mediocre terms that could be used to describe this long-term relationship morass people find themselves in – why?

In this book, these questions are answered through taking a hard look at the conventional relationship theories and exploring where these classic theories come up short. After reviewing past relationship wisdom, I found it provides well intended, yet incomplete, advice for those looking for a truly successful long term partner. For example, many popular relationship books and teachings stress concepts such as:

- Love, communication, trust and connection
- Understanding that men and women are different
- Be mindful of each other
- Understanding the stage of your relationship
- "Rules" for relationships
- Habits for successful relationships
- Relationship languages

These prior teachings are stand-alone concepts that are perfectly valid as an individual concept, yet they all miss the crucial integrated concept that they are all unknowingly based upon. None of these classic relationship concepts can be truly successful unless they are based upon the core Unified Theory of Relationship Success concept described in this book. Conversely, if your relationship is formed from the Unified Theory of Relationship Success, then all the classic relationship advice and teachings will be spectacularly successful! In other words, the Unified Theory of Relationship Success provides the core relationship concept enabling all prior teachings to be successful in your life.

Prior to Einstein and his Theory of Relativity ($E=MC^2$) published in 1905, there were multiple theories in the physics world regarding how energy, matter and time interact in the physical world. In the years before Einstein, scientists had developed theories related to how energy works, separate theories related to how matter works, and still other theories related to how time works.

An excellent analogy for the connection between classic relationship concepts and The Unified Theory of Relationship Success is Einstein's theory of relativity. Prior to Einstein and his Theory of Relativity (published in 1901), there were multiple concepts in the physics world regarding how energy, matter and time operate in the physical world. Yet nobody understood how they are related and observed. Brilliantly, in a simple three page paper, Einstein described the basic relationships between energy, matter and time which took the physics world by storm, and laid the groundwork for all modern physics concepts.

Similary, The Unified Theory of Relationship Success connects the stand-alone classic relationship success concepts with a unifying solid base. This resulting solid relationship base in your life allows the classic relationship success concepts to spontaneously appear, thrive and flourish into a lifelong successful relationship.

Just as Einstein did with this Theory of Relativity, in this book we develop the thoughts contained in classic relationship teachings into an integrated concept for relationship success.

For years people have tried to understand and define the spiritual, physical, emotional and intellectual complexities of human relationships. Thousands of authors, speakers, scientists and spiritualists have attempted to identify or describe the individual components within a successful spiritual, emotional, physical and intellectual relationship with your partner. Some authors have focused upon spiritual components, others have focused upon physical needs, others have focused on emotional components, and still others have focused upon intellectual components.

As result, hundreds of books, conferences and teachings are available to us regarding how to have a successful lifelong relationship with each book focusing on a couple of the four physical, intellectual, emotional and spiritual components of a successful relationship. Each of these relationship components is not individualistic and unique, they are inter-related and complex, which is why successful relationships are inter-related and complex. Many people have identified that these exist and are important; however none have identified how these develop, interact and are fostered in a successful relationship.

Just as Einstein did with his Theory of Relativity, the purpose of this book is to unite all of the classic individual physical, intellectual, emotional and spiritual relationship theories into a single elegantly simple theory -

The Unified Theory of Relationship Success

Since this unified theory is simple, composed of three rules and then a unifying Theory governing how the rules interact, anyone can use it to provide clarity for their individual relationship goals and also to help find the perfect partner with whom to create and sustain a lifelong successful relationship full of love, happiness, communication, trust and kindness.

CHAPTER TWO
Traditional relationship thinking gets it backward

The genesis of the Unified Theory is that I realized traditional relationship thinking gets it backward

All the previously mentioned traditional/classical concepts for a successful relationship such as

- Love, communication, trust and connection
- Understanding that men and women are different
- Be mindful of each other
- Understanding the stage of your relationship
- "Rules" for relationships
- Habits for successful relationships
- Relationship languages

…..are really secondary concepts to a successful relationship. The antiquated philosophy that anybody can have a successful relationship if they simply focus on adding more of these types of concepts to their relationship is false.

Let me repeat. The classical and outdated concept that the foundation of a successful relationship comes from concepts like love, trust, communication, and support is antiquated, false and backward.

Wow! How could that be? Don't they fall into any successful relationship?

The answer is yes, of course!

However, the key misunderstanding is that concepts such as love, trust, communication, and support are not the FOCUS of a successful relationship, they are the NATURAL BYPRODUCTS of a successful relationship, and are created and defined by the two partners on the same path in the relationship. In other words, traditional relationship advice got it backwards. It is impossible for these types of relationship concepts to be responsible for developing a successful relationship on their own with partners on different paths.

It is futile for an individual partner to add more love, communication, support and honesty to the relationship if the other partner is on a separate path - it simply won't work because you're going in different directions. It would be like moving a shade loving plant into the sun because you think it needs more light to grow and flourish. You think you're helping the plant, but the plant does not want/need/understand what you are doing to it, and may even shrivel and pull away as a result of your well-intended actions.

Conversely if you're both on the same path, your mutual experiences naturally create an ever-deepening sense of mutual love, trust communication and honesty in the relationship which continually deepens over your lifetime. Neither of you are intentionally adding these wonderful components of a successful relationship; they are being organically grown within your relationship! Taking a look at the previous plant example, now you are on the same path and you move the plant to a nicely shaded location because you understand it needs the shade. Here the plant thrives, growing into a beautiful expression of life – both you and the plant are happy, and thrive together because you both are getting what you need from the relationship.

The great news: A successful relationship stemming from two people on the same path will easily and organically develop these types of love, trust, communication, and support concepts.

CHAPTER THREE
What is a successful relationship?

But first - what is a successful relationship? This Unified Theory applies to any kind of a relationship; it could be two drug addicts on the street or two college love birds, both of whose relationship lasts a lifetime. The focus of the Unified Theory is to help you find the most successful relationship of your lifetime – as you and your partner define it. To judge the accuracy of the Unified Theory, it was applied to multiple relationships where I had knowledge of the partner's background. Some of which stayed together and some of which have broken up. It correctly predicted both cases. You can now use this new tool to develop and grow a relationship which is ultimately long-term successful on the terms both you and your partner desire.

When asked what forms the basis of a successful relationship, women typically answer- honesty, loyalty and communication, while men typically answer- sex and respect. We will see later on how these answers are really not the basis of a successful relationship unless the partners are on the same path and have the same toolbox of emotional skills to create reciprocal trust, loyalty, communication, sex and respect.

When someone sees an exquisitely beautiful woman, or a stunningly handsome man, why isn't there a lifelong successful relationship immediately formed? That initial chemistry should be enough.... right? WRONG Although great for propagating the species, this initial genetic animal attraction is no guarantee of a successful relationship.

Successful relationships are formed deep in the emotional minds of you and your partner, from similar experiences that create the path that you're on in life, giving each of you a similar emotional toolkit. Then, when you do meet you are both well equipped, with a similar toolbox filled with the tools each of you need to support the emotional, physical and intellectual needs of the other. This then creates a successful life-long relationship defined on the terms you define from your mutual path.

Both your path and your partners path in life were created by the people and experiences surrounding you from an early age, and a successful relationship involves finding another person with similar experiences and thus a similar path in life. This doesn't mean you actually share the literal experiences which created each of your paths, in other words if you like skydiving, you don't have to find another skydiver. Or if you like sewing, your partner doesn't have to like sewing.

However, as we will see in the following pages, you and your partner will naturally share the figurative experiences which developed the path you are both on.

Applying The Unified Theory of Relationship Success learned in this book will allow you to identify and create the perfect relationship for both you and your partner, resulting in that elusive successful relationship bursting with long-term love, trust, communication, commitment, sex and respect.

As defined in this book, your successful relationship is a relationship between you and your partner where you both participate, laugh, love, conspire, cry, support, communicate, continuously physically and emotionally connect, derive enjoyment and look forward to the next day together. If this is your vision of a successful relationship, welcome aboard!

Now let's learn about the Unified Theory and how to apply it!

Just as Einstein looked at rules for time, matter and energy and then combined them. We will take a look at the three successful relationship rules, and then combine them into the single Unified Theory governing how they interact with each other.

CHAPTER FOUR

Rule 1: Physical Attraction

The first rule is that of physical attraction. This rule is the weakest of the three rules, and it states that for a couple to bond and persevere in a successful relationship there must be some level of initial purely physical attraction.

This attraction does not have to be the instantaneous OMG he/she is the most beautiful/handsome person I have ever met, let's make love! AKA "Love at first sight" attraction. That is a holdover from our "propagating the species" genetic programming, and rarely lasts over a multi-decade relationship.

The reason this is the weakest of the three rules, is because physical attraction is easiest to degrade in importance over time as it becomes overshadowed by the presence of the remaining two rules in the relationship.

However, the critical importance of the rule of physical attraction is that this rule initially allows the other two rules the opportunity to actually create your successful relationship! If you don't like what you see, you will move on and never get to the following two rules, however if you like or love what you see you will stay around to give the other two rules time to be applied.

In other words, the rule of physical attraction acts like a catalyst to facilitate the emotional bonding you and your partner will experience within the other two rules.

The rule of physical attraction simply states that, initially and then over time, when you physically view your partner, you like what you see! This may seem like somewhat of a low threshold, however it is initially critical to a successful relationship. As previously mentioned, if you don't physically like what you initially see in a potential partner, you will move on and there is no chance the remaining two rules would have an opportunity to create a successful relationship!

However, if you have positive emotions toward your partner's physical appearance at initial introduction and then follow-on time together, the rule has been met and the catalyst for a lifelong successful relationship is doing its job.

CHAPTER FIVE

Rule 2: Everyone Has A Path

The second rule in the unified theory of relationship success is that everybody has a path. Your path is the sum of your consistent life experiences, desires, hopes, dreams, and emotions. It is your naturally consistent set of values, demeanor, and level of engagement in life.

This is the hardest part in a successful relationship - actually figuring out who you are and what path you're on. Doing this involves lots of introspection and selfishness because if you're not going deep in yourself and being as selfish as you can to support yourself, you have no idea what path you are on and have no idea how to find a partner on that path.

Your path was typically formed by you and your village, when you were in elementary or middle school, and you have been on that path ever since.

Now, let's not get too focused here - your path is not a narrow trail like a hiking trail in the mountains. Your path is more like a multi-lane freeway winding through the world, yet always going in a single general direction - not a literal/physical direction but more of an imaginary direction such as west-up, or perhaps down-north. It is formed from the components of whom you have consistently been, are and will be physically, emotionally, spiritually and intellectually if there were no external influences pulling and pushing you in other directions.

Your path is composed of those characteristics in your life that have been consistent from an early age, and remain part of your life today. For example, perhaps from an early age you always liked reading books, and continue to enjoy relaxing in a quiet space with a good novel. This consistent activity forms reading books as a component of your path. In another example, perhaps you always liked adrenaline activities like jumping out of trees, rock climbing, racing motorcycles, and you still pursue those activities today. These consistent activities form adrenaline activities as a component of your path.

For another example, perhaps from an early age you have always been a very empathetic and caring person who supports others. This consistent emotional space in your life forms an empathetic and caring component of your path.

Remember, your path is composed of spiritual, physical, emotional and intellectual components consistent THROUGHOUT your life. If you decide that learning to paint would be fun one weekend, that is not part of your path, it is merely a point in time. Or, if you decide that 3 months of world travel would be interesting, that is not your path, it just another point in time.

As we will see later, identifying your path and the components that create your path, is the single most important activity you can undertake in developing a successful relationship with another person. It is critically important for you to take the time and spend the energy to become well-grounded and deeply rooted in yourself, and thus identify your path - before you can create a successful relationship with another.

CHAPTER SIX
Your Village Shapes Your Path

Your village is crucial to the success of your long-term relationship. It provides you with the emotional tools required to function on your path and then for you to both give and receive emotional support to your partner in a successful relationship.

Everybody is a member of their own small village. This village is comprised of the people around you, people that you grew up with, your parents, your friends, your teachers, your schools, your experiences, and could even include fictional cartoon/movie/storybook characters you consistently identify with. This village then forms the path that you are on, and develops the set of emotional tools within your emotional toolbox, which you then use on a daily basis to interact with others, and most importantly - your partner.

The emotions, values, perceptions, philosophies and self-image you develop are the result of processing information provided to you by all of the people and experiences in your village. This provides a sense of security, just as in herd animals grouping together with common needs, wants, desires and goals.

For example, perhaps your parents taught you formal table manners and to pass the full plates of food around - or perhaps you simply learned to eat as fast as you could because the food would be gone before you're full. In the first example inner security and peace are developed within your emotional toolbox, and in the second example, inner insecurities and competition are developed in your emotional toolbox. Unless quickly eliminated, these emotional tools then become part of your lifelong emotional toolkit.

In another scenario, perhaps your teachers throughout the years told you they believed in you, you are amazing and can do anything. Or perhaps they ignored your requests for help, ask you to sit in places you couldn't hear in the classroom, and didn't provide constructive feedback on your homework.

In the first scenario you learn self-worth and self-esteem as an emotional tool, in the second example you are instilled with doubt and insecurity as emotional tools. Unless quickly eliminated, these emotional tools then become part of your lifelong emotional toolkit.

If you have been shown love and support your entire life you have love and support as an emotional tool.

If you've been shown neglect and abuse your entire life you have neglect and abuse as an emotional tool.

If you've been shown inclusion and participation all your life, you have inclusion and participation as emotional tools. If you've been shown isolation and non-participation throughout your life you have isolation and non-participation as emotional tools. If you've been shown empathy and kindness throughout your life, you have empathy and kindness as emotional tools. If you've been shown apathy and meanness throughout your life you have apathy and meanness as emotional tools.

Each village experience you have - with your family, with the friends you choose, with your sports teammates, with your school teachers - develops your brains' emotional pathways to respond in a particular manner, which is what then forms your emotional toolkit. This is why surrounding yourself with the correct people and developing the right village to provide and support the appropriate emotional tools for your path is crucial to a successful long-term relationship.

Eventually you become the village and the village becomes you, and you synergistically feed ideas and information from one another; however these ideas and experiences are all within the mutual village norm. Your emotional toolbox has been filled by the village and the village can't provide additional tools because it has already provided you all the available emotional tools within the village.

These village provided emotional tools are initially all you have to use on your path, and in a perfect world, they are the only tools you would need to have a successful relationship. However, these tools are given to you by your village members and these village members have their own individual paths. Their tools may work on their individual path; however the tools they give you may not be the emotional tools you require on your individual path.

Accordingly, pursuing self-aware self-centeredness for a while may be required in order for you to internally and organically develop new emotional tools that work on your path, and also for you to realize which old legacy emotional tools should be filed away in a box never to be used again. For example if you have been taught apathy as an emotional response to an issue, yet you realize on your path empathy and kindness work better. You need to find a village to learn empathy and kindness, and then put that in your emotional toolkit and file apathy away. Or, if you've been taught instant anger is the appropriate response to a problem, yet you find your path works better with a quiet response, you need to find a village where you can learn how to respond to problems calmly and quietly. Then add this new calm emotional tool to your tool kit and file the anger tool away, never to be used again.

Your original village is the starting space for your life and what formed your path, however it is still a village and you are a voluntary member of the village. If your experiences are good, you have all the emotional tools you need for your path, and you have a successful relationship - great! Then you can continue with your village activities and live a strong life.

Alternately, if your village hasn't provided the emotional tools you need both for your path, and you are struggling to find a successful relationship, you can always leave the village and find a new village with new emotional tools more appropriate for your path.

You'll have the tools from your old village forever but a new village will allow you to develop the new emotional tools that you need on your individual path. Old emotional tools that don't work on your path can then be left behind and replaced in your toolbox by new emotional tools more useful on your individual path.

Moving out of your village is scary and unnerving since you no longer have the infrastructure and support of the people surrounding you. This entire legacy supporting infrastructure now needs to be recreated to define your new village and develop new tools for your new tool box. In parallel, members of your old village may experience a sense of loss at your leaving and react negatively towards you or your new experiences. This is to be expected. Hopefully you're old village members will support your new endeavors, however recognize that they may not know how to emotionally support you because your emotional requirements are different than their village infrastructure can provide - which is the reason you left in the first place. So they may not know how to emotionally support your new journey.

The bottom line is that your village provides your emotional tools, and thereby your capacity to successfully relate to your partner on your mutual path. If you're not having successful relationships, check your emotional toolbox and see if the contents are in line with your path. If they are not, find a new village to provide you with the missing emotional tools for your toolbox to be used along the path you and your partner share.

Sharing this emotional toolbox along your mutual path enables you and your partner to understand how to emotionally support one another and create a successful lifelong relationship filled with love, trust, communication, kindness, sex, respect and all the other path components you both desire.

CHAPTER SEVEN
How Your Path Works

Your path is composed of multiple lanes, some slow and some fast. You can change lanes on your path, sometimes the slow lane is desired, and sometimes the fast lane is more appropriate for you. But you're still going in that same general direction on your path, and developing the same emotional tools in your toolbox along that path.

It's important to understand that your path is composed of components from your past, present, and anticipated future, also your village, and your experiences along the way. It is not enough to simply understand who you are right now, because that is a contrived point in time, and is of limited help identifying your path or your perfect partnership. As an analogy, let's pretend you are blindfolded and driven to a four-way intersection on a country road where your blindfold is taken off and you are ask to find your way home. You know where you are right now - you're at the intersection of two country roads, however you have no idea how you got there or where you're going. Thus simply knowing where you are at that moment does little good on your travel, and you have no idea how to get home.

Now let's take that same example but you use Google maps and figure out interesting things that you would like to see along the way and where that road is taking you. You start the journey and come to that same intersection of two country roads. Knowing the information about where you came from and where the road goes, you can easily find your way home from there.

When you are on your natural path, your mind and body are energized and engaged with life. Your dreams, desires and hopes have a tendency to materialize as you travel down the path. You have found your "happy place", which is really just a natural expression of you on your path.

When you are not on your natural path, your physical and spiritual self is constrained, you are doing things that are unnatural to you and that create friction and angst in your mental state.

For example, let's say your father was a computer engineer and you were trained by him to be a computer engineer, and you went to school to be a computer engineer and you found a good job as a computer engineer but there was always something missing in your life and work experience. Then one day you take a coffee roasting, grinding and brewing class and realize that is your inner passion. You decide to start a coffee business, and now your life flourishes and you are happy. This newfound passion uses your same computer engineer skill sets of logic and precision, but they are now applied to a sensory aromatic and tactile product which is where your path actually led. You had the correct tools (logic, precision) all along, yet your village was requiring you to apply them on the wrong path (computer engineer) which created angst and friction in your mental state, yet you didn't know why. The reason was you were not following your path.

Your path is composed of whom you: were, are and will be. It also contains the emotional tools you have available to relate to others. All these components combine to create the true story of you - your path - which you can then use to find the right partner and develop a successful lifelong relationship filled with love, joy, communication, honesty, respect, and any other components you mutually desire!

Now, having established the relationship between your village, your path and your emotional toolkit, the traditional concept that a successful relationship is simply built upon love, trust, communication and support is incomplete. All these concepts are missing the basis they are all derived from – your path. This is the critical importance of determining your own path, and the components within your path.

CHAPTER EIGHT

How To Find Your Path

Now that we have established the importance of your path to a successful relationship, the most crucial step is to identify what path you are on!

Your path is the direction you're moving in life, the essence of you in life, and contains all of the emotional tools you have available to relate to your partner. Absent mind altering drugs or physical brain damage, your path has not, and will not, change. You have been on this path since you were 10 years old.

Luckily, you're not the only person on your path; your path is not unique to you like your fingerprint. If it was, the world would rarely have successful relationships since two people would never be on the same path and thus would not have the necessary emotional tools to resolve differences, develop new experiences, and create a successful relationship bond.

Instead your path is filled with others also in their natural unbounded human state, going in the same direction as you, perhaps not in the same lane at a specific moment in time but on the same path, and traveling in the same direction as you.

Your path is how you would think, feel and act if you were free from external constraints and pressures. It's your natural human state or condition, and the resulting movement of that unbounded condition through the world. This consistent past, present and future movement of your unbounded condition throughout life creates the path that you're on. You will continue on that path your entire life.

For example, if you really liked playing and watching soccer when you were young, and continue to like playing and watching soccer today - one of the components of your path is to have time to play and watch soccer in your life. In other words, if you had no external pressures from your career, friends, family and your village, you would prioritize playing and watching soccer into your life and this characteristic becomes part of the path you have taken since you were 10 years old.

Your path is composed of multiple components, or characteristics, operating in parallel to form the core essence of who you are, how you act, what you think, and how you feel when free of the external influence of your village. To define the components of your path, it is necessary to take a self-aware, selfish deep dive into your past, present and future to find the characteristics which have remained consistent throughout your life. This is your path, and you must be selfish to determine it.

Selfishness is good.

Not self-centered selfishness, but self-aware selfishness. Self-centered selfishness forms the classic individualistic, narcissistic "I am the center of the universe" traits. These rarely play well in a successful relationship, since by definition, how can two self-centered, narcissistic, "I am the center of the universe" people have a successful unified relationship?

On the other hand, self-aware selfishness is required for you to know your path, and to then understand when somebody else is on that same path. Spending time doing, thinking, and acting as only you want to allows you to understand what you about and want to do. Give yourself time and space for self-reflection by temporarily moving out, and away from, the external village influences.

"Actions speak louder than words". That phrase is applicable both to others and internally to yourself. It's important to take long periods of time to do things only for your benefit, shutting others out and letting your inner soul express itself. The actions and emotions you experience when you are being self-aware selfish are actually your path presenting itself to you for inspection. The more self-aware selfish time you spend, the clearer your path becomes. You can then start to evaluate if you have the right emotional tools for the path, develop missing ones, and discard antiquated ones. Once you experience self-aware selfishness, and understand your path, you can then more easily evaluate other people's paths and find that single life partner on your path - consummating in a successful lifelong relationship.

In other words, to have a successful life relationship with somebody on your path and then change together on that path, you have to be as self-aware selfish as possible as often as possible until you know your path and can then also evaluate other people's paths to see if they are on your path. This is why periods of self-aware selfishness are critical to understanding your path and then the path of others.

So…. Ignore the advice and admonitions of your friends, family, co-workers and go spend time doing the things only you want to do, experiencing the experiences only you want to, living the emotions only you want to, creating your physical appearance as only you want to.

Once you've had enough of those self-aware selfish experiences, you will find out who you are and thus the crucial components of your path. Only at this time can you understand the fullness of your path, and how to understand if someone else is on that same path.

Your path characteristics include the following:

(Note - I have included example questions to ask yourself within each characteristic, there are many more which you can define for yourself – after all, your path is composed of who you are and is not limited to the few questions you read in this book)

Moral Characteristics:
- What has stayed constant in your moral beliefs over the years?
- What moral characteristics do you hold most important?
- How often do moral considerations come into your decision making?

Physical Characteristics:
- How do you view exercise?
- What image do you have of your physical self?
- What physical traits have you consistently been drawn to in your partners?

Emotional Characteristics:
- What are your strongest emotions?
- How often do you display emotions?
- How do you view a display of emotions?

Happiness Characteristics:
- What gives you joy in life?
- How often to you feel happy?
- How does being around other happy/sad people affect you?

Artistic Characteristics:
- How often do you express artistic creativity?
- What do you feel when others express their creativity around you?
- How important is it to have the ability to express yourself artistically?

Intellectual Characteristics:
- How do you view yourself in the intellectual world?
- How do you feel regarding deep conversations requiring significant thought?
- When others exhibit intellectual characteristics, how do you feel?

Lifestyle Characteristics:
- Do you feel more comfortable with a structured lifestyle, or a more casual lifestyle?
- What type of sleeping patterns do you prefer – early riser or night owl?
- What type of foods do you prefer – vegetarian, omnivore?

Sexual Characteristics:
- How do you view intimacy?
- Is sexual intimacy a crucial part of a relationship, or a necessary component?
- What types of sexual intimacy have you always liked best?

Social Characteristics:
- Do you prefer to be the life of the party, or sit back and observe social gatherings?
- How comfortable are you in public social settings?
- What types of social groups and memberships have you joined?

Work Characteristics:
- What are your work habits?
- How do you view work?
- If you were not working, what activities would you be doing?

Family Characteristics:
- How important is a close family to you?
- What type of family interaction is most important to you?
- What actions do you take to create/maintain family bonds?

All of these characteristics are present in your path. The characteristics creating your path are those that you find consistently showing up throughout your life, or they would show up if your village was not repressing them. Remember, your path characteristics are those that you find important regardless of the influence from other members of your village. They are you, unbounded.

CHAPTER NINE

How To Know If Someone Is On Your Path

Ok, I have spent enough self-aware selfish time and know my path - but how do I know what path somebody else is on?

Finding the perfect person for you, who is on your path, is now a focused matter of evaluating the other person through the eyes of your path. This needs to be done openly and honestly, and outside of how sexually attracted you are to them. The sexual attraction initially plays a huge role in pulling people together (see Rule #1), and can easily overwhelm obvious indicators the other person is not on your path.

Asking friends, co-workers, family members if the person is right for you does not help. Of course you can take their comments into consideration; however you have to do this path analysis on the other person independently, by yourself. All your village members are on their own paths, thus they don't have the ability to understand your path and the path of your potential lifelong partner. This is something only you can do once you know your own path. You determine if they're on your path through evaluating their past, present, and future wants, needs and desires to see if they align with your path.

Take the time to ask your partner questions regarding their early life, their present life, and where their future is headed. Look for clues from their words and actions; consistently mentioned items give you clues to the components of their path.

Have they always loved tattoos? Have they always disliked pets? Is knitting something they have consistently done? Just like you, these consistent items in their history form components of their path. In this example, your potential partners path has always, and will be, composed of tattoos, no animals, and knitting.

You can then check for similarities with your path, both obvious non-negotiable components, and also "unrealized" components of their path which are in your path.

The first evaluation of your potential partners' path is to identify the non-negotiable components of your path.

Non-negotiable path components form the building blocks of your path, those items that you absolutely and completely - in your core self- believe to be true about you and have to be available, (or absent as the case may be) in your partner. These non-negotiable components are the core things you believe, feel, do, and desire. They compose the essence of who you were, are and will be. These non-negotiable characteristics simply have to be in your partner's path for the relationship to work. Once you have identified your non-negotiable path components, the next step is very straightforward - take a look to see if they are present or absent in your potential partners life.

For example, perhaps you find your path includes non-smoking as a non-negotiable characteristic, and then another characteristic such as an enjoyment of cooking. If a potential partner smokes, there's absolutely no way you would establish any sort of a relationship with them. If you went to an online dating profile and it says they smoke, they immediately get deleted. If you see an attractive potential partner in a social gathering, and then they pull out a cigarette, you immediately lose interest. In summary, your non-negotiables are the first cut in eliminating many people not on your path.

In this circumstance, to have a successful relationship, your partner MUST not smoke since it is a non-negotiable. Once you get through all the non-negotiable path components, then move down your path list to the less black and white path components and evaluate if your potential partner has those in their life. Hopefully all of your remaining path characteristics are also obviously present in your partner's path. However, odds are that they are not directly present, but the good news is that if you can combine a couple of your remaining path characteristics to match a characteristic in your partner's path, your relationship will still be successful. However, if any of your non-negotiable characteristics or remaining characteristics (even when combined) cannot be found in your partner's path, your relationship will continue to struggle.

With these remaining components of your path, remember that your path components may actually be in your potential partners path but yet "unrealized". Returning to our previous example regarding the love of cooking on your path – your potential partner doesn't need to have an initial enjoyment of cooking if they have related characteristics in their path such as an inquisitive mind and love of food. Those inquisitive mind and love of food characteristics on their path could then be combined to create and ignite an enjoyment of cooking on your mutual path. However, if your potential partner simply hates how food tastes, smells and feels, the love of cooking characteristic of your path will never be present in their path, you are not on the same path, and your relationship will continue to struggle.

In another example, perhaps you are addicted to bungee jumping as part of your path, and meet a potential partner who's never bungee jumped but likes to downhill race mountain bikes and has an inquisitive mind. The downhill mountain bike racing and the inquisitive mind can easily activate the unrealized bungee jumping component of their path, and become a component of your mutual successful path!

However, if you can't find a combination of their path components that could be activated to match yours, it's still a no-go, and time to keep looking for that one person who is definitely out there to make the rest of your mutual lives a successful relationship.

In summary, you know somebody is on your path, when all of your non-negotiable components are immediately present in their path and your remaining path components are either present or can be activated in your partners' path. This process involves a lot of deep discussions between you and your future partner, a great excuse to spend quality time together!

CHAPTER TEN

What Happens When Paths Cross?

With everybody having a path, and many paths weaving through the world, once you understand your path it's easy to see what paths other people are on, and you have amazing clarity in the relationship world. But there's also an interesting situation:

With so many paths in the world weaving around, what happens when they cross?

When you're on your path you know where it's going and where it's been - it's a continuous line; and you understand other people's paths are also a continuous line. These paths may never intersect and you can watch them and understand them but they never cross just like two parallel lines drawn on a sheet of paper. You could keep drawing those parallel lines in the direction they're going on that sheet of paper forever and they would never cross, they would always be two lines separated by a distance.... forever.

For example, from your path, you can watch the path of a famous movie star unfold. You can read news reports regarding them, you can watch them in movies, and you may even see them walking down the street somewhere. Your path and their's are simply wandering through the world, you take notice of theirs yet they may not take notice of yours. There's no significant interaction but you're aware they exist. Your parallel paths will go on forever, as part of the learning process of life.

Now let's take the situation when you start doodling on that piece of paper, and you start drawing a curvy line from the lower left to the upper right and a second doodle creates another line going from the lower right to the upper left corner of the paper. Somewhere in the middle of that white piece of paper, those two lines will cross each other and intersect at a point, and then keep going in different directions forever.

Similarly, your personal path will cross with the paths of many others. This is inevitable as you go through your life meeting new people - you meet both them and their path. Upon initial meeting, you have two choices: 1) choose to accept them into your village, let them be one of the influencers in your life, and possibly your lifelong partner or 2) you reject them as not relevant or appropriate for your village and self, and thus they don't participate in your life any further.

If you make the decision to reject them from your village, there is no crossing of paths, simply two paths that bounce off each other. An example is a quick conversation with the grocery clerk while checking out and you find you have a mutual interest in a television show - then you pick up your groceries and go home. Or a conversation with another parent at the playground where are you find your kids had a mutual teacher three years ago, then you collect your child and head to the dentist. There's no further interaction or thought put into those types of meetings. Your paths bounce off of each other.

But what happens when you accept them into your life as a village member or potential partner?

At that time, your paths actually cross. The two pencil lines on the white sheet of paper actually cross at the intersection or point. Your path and their path have a point in common. Forever.

The basis for this point in common could be any of the mutual components in each of your two individual paths. For example you need a great laboratory technician who is easy to get along with, and this person is a great laboratory technician with a warm and charming personality, who happens to like board games as much as you do. You develop a friendship beyond the lab, playing board games, and start to consider them as your partner.

Or in another example, you meet somebody on the ski lift who is a great skier (as you are also), they live somewhat close, and you both love tacos. You decide to spend more time pursuing skiing and tacos together. You develop a relationship based upon skiing and tacos and start to consider them as your partner.

These crossed-path connections are how our lives, friends and relationships grow and expand.

Now, here's the tricky part...when you meet the other person at that crossed point, does this mean you are on their path and they are on your path? You have many path components in common, they seem nice, you are physically attracted to them, etc.... On 1st blush, this could be "The One"! Perfect for you, finally! The search is over......

That's why this is so tricky; it's fraught with DANGER.... You are not on the same path. For a point in time, you have many components of your individual paths in common, but their path will continually draw them in their direction while your path will continually draw you in your direction. As time moves forward you will find yourselves farther and farther apart, bewildered that: "how could this person I met when he/she was so perfect be so different now?" What happened?

Initially, everything seems perfectly aligned. You are flush with attraction, excited because of the commonalities, and looking forward to the future with this person. You typically focus on the obvious components you have in common and mutually pursue those - both of you are having a great time! You are running off on ski trip after ski trip, or spending hours playing board games into the wee hours of the morning following your lab work. This is actually the perfect person to have as a long term member of your village, NOT "The" perfect person to have as your ultimately successful relationship.

What??

You are not on the same path; you are simply sharing a point in time. You are at the intersection of those two lines on that white sheet of paper that continue in different directions forever. The point that you are both sharing will eventually be history in your path and also theirs.

Since you're at a point and not on the same path, there is no mutual growth from that point - they don't become your successful relationship partner because they can't!

Since they're not on your path, they don't have the emotional toolkit to support you, just as you do not have the appropriate emotional toolkit to support them. Inevitably they simply become a member of your village, and you become a member of theirs. This relationship degradation happens regardless of whether you are either single or married, regardless of whether you both felt the relationship started out as mutually loving, caring, compassionate, and kind. This relationship degradation may take a month or 5 years, but it's inevitable since you are not on the same path and your individual paths are drawing you apart.

This is the trap that many people fall into when initially setting up a long term relationship or getting married. They meet somebody who is "perfect" at a point in time, quickly connect with them and then grow apart as their paths separate, inevitably becoming members of each other's village rather than growing together into a single unified successful relationship. This leads to mutual frustration, bewilderment, sadness and other emotional issues that challenge and ultimately fracture the relationship.

So, in summary - when looking at a potential partner, it's crucial to identify whether or not your paths are crossing, or you're actually on the same path. The first is an intersection - a point - with a high probability of negative relational issues in the future - you are best as village friends. However, if you are on the same path – watch out world! A successful relationship just walked into your life, and a spectacular lifetime of love, caring, trust, communication, respect, excitement and bonding awaits!

However you both mutually decide to create it, your unified path relationship will be spectacularly successful!

CHAPTER ELEVEN
Rule 3: Everyone Is Changing, Including You

The third rule in The Unified Theory of Relationship Success is that everybody is continuously changing. Everybody includes people around you: your loved ones, your family, your co-workers, and you.....everybody.

It's important to internalize that you, and your partner, are constantly changing. The self-image you have right now is not the same self-image you had 5, 10 or 15 years ago. You, and your partner, are not defined by where you are now because you will be inevitably changing in the future. Watch out for labeling someone with a static snapshot.

For example, when you meet a waiter in a restaurant, your brain instantly snapshots that person as "a waiter" to freeze and categorize them at a moment in time, and when you see them the next day in the grocery store you think "there is that waiter". By default our brain snapshots everyone. This is a natural response to the inability of our brains to understand the complex lives of everyone we meet. There is no way our brains can fully learn and remember all the physical, emotional, spiritual and intellectual nuances of everyone we meet throughout our lives. Thus, we snapshot label "the waiter", "the professor", "the housewife", "the runner", "the mechanic" etc.

However, in reality that waiter/professor/housewife/runner/mechanic and partner is actually changing as you snapshot them and could actually be in college studying to be a doctor, or traveling through town on their way to start a new career as a social worker, or creating an amazing artistic mural downtown. Beware of the snapshot as a people label, people are constantly changing and evolving.

Similarly, your relationship partner was, is and will be changing. This is equally as critical to internalize, that they cannot be snapshot labeled. Once again, both you and your partner will be changing as you move into the future.

CHAPTER TWELVE

The Unified Theory of Relationship Success

Now that we have developed the three individual rules for a successful relationship, what do they mean when combined? The Unified Theory of Relationship Success combines the three rules into a clear path you can use to find a successful relationship for the rest of your life.

The Unified Theory of Relationship Success combines the three rules as follows:

A SUCCESSFUL RELATIONSHIP =

PHYSICAL ATTRACTION (Rule #1)
+
SAME PATH(Rule #2)
+
MUTUAL CHANGE(Rule #3)

In other words, find a partner you have some continued level of physical attraction to, and who is on your path - and then understand that you are both changing along that path.

When you accomplish this your relationship will be successful.

Why?

Because, when you find somebody whose path has the same components as your path, you have similar emotional tool kits and have the capacity to understand your partner on more than a physical level. You now know how they like to receive and give support, communication, love, and affection because it's similar to the way you like to receive those same relationship expressions. Similarly, you know how to interpret their expressions of communications, love, support, and affection that you receive. Over time you become a harmonious partnership that is everlasting and fulfilling for both parties.

In other words, being on the same path allows both parties to enhance and complement each other by using similar emotional tools to communicate. This is how a deep selfless love, or agape love, becomes possible in a successful relationship. When on the same path, partners are "in tune" with each other and each constantly recognize and address small issues before they become larger issues.

Within your Unified Theory based relationship, all of the prior classic concepts of a successful relationship such as communication, trust, connection, mindfulness, understanding your relationship stage, relationship habits, and relationship languages then appear and grow both naturally and effortlessly. This is because you are both on the same path, have a similar emotional toolkit, and understand how to emotionally connect with your partner. The Unified Theory provides your relationship with the healthy and solid baseline from which all the classic successful relationship concepts will spontaneously emerge and flourish.

Partners on the same path in a successful relationship will periodically fall out of balance in favor of one or the other. Assuming the partners are on the same path and have the same emotional toolbox, the out of balance moments then provide mutual opportunities for each partner to enhance the relationship by exhibiting love, warmth, care, support and encouragement in the moment.

Conversely, if you're not on the same path with your partner, you don't have the appropriate emotional tools to provide love trust, communication, support etc in the manner that your partner can effectively receive them. Similarly, you can't receive love, trust, communication, support etc from your partner in the way that you require to effectively process them. So if you're not on the same path you have two people trying to do the right thing in the relationship, but not having the emotional tools and skill sets to accomplish this. So it becomes a futile act which then builds apathy, boredom and resentment over time.

For example, let's say you and your partner are not on the same path, thus it's not a successful relationship. You are on a hypothetical up-west freeway path and your partner is on a hypothetical right-south freeway path. You have an issue come up - a flat tire. You call your partner on the right-south freeway and tell them you have a flat tire and need help. Your partner says, "okay I'll call AAA", they do, and your tire gets fixed. Then that night you're angry with your partner because your emotional toolkit wanted your partner to come and be with you and fix the tire or stay with you while the tire was fixed - and they didn't. At the same time your right-south partner is frustrated with you because their emotional toolkit said they did what you asked them to do to - get the car fixed. Although they didn't do it themselves, their emotional toolkit found no need to come and do it themselves. Thus your relationship continues strained, frustrated and disjointed. This happens repeatedly throughout your time together until you both get so frustrated that you throw up your hands, and the relationship ends.

Now let's take that same example, however both you and your partner are on the same path - the west-up freeway in life. Accordingly, you have a successful lifelong relationship and share similar emotional tools in your mutual toolkit. Your tire goes flat on the freeway and you call your partner to let them know your tire is flat and you need help. Having the same tools in your emotional toolkit because you're on the same path, your partner wants to come and help you. They immediately turn around and come to your aid by calling AAA with you. Your tire gets fixed. Then you both drive off and come home for dinner that night. Around the table you're both talking about how happy you are to have supported each other during that issue earlier in the day, and your relationship bond grows closer and deepens. This happens over and over throughout your life, and each challenge eventually creates a deeper bond between you and your partner in your successful relationship!

The third critical aspect of the Unified Theory is to continually implement Rule #3 and realize that both of you are changing. Once you find the partner on your path, the changes you and your partner make are all related to your path. You don't change paths. Your changes include the speed at which you and your partner move down your lanes, and the lanes that you and your partner are in on your mutual path. All of your changes relate to your position on your path but you're still going in the same direction, however the speed and lane may vary at any time.

For example, perhaps for the last year-and-a-half you've been a hard-charging corporate executive on your path, and then your project ends, and you decide to take two months off to follow a band around Europe before your next project starts. Have you gone nuts? Definitely not! You simply changed from the fast lane to the slow lane of your path for a while. However you're going in the same direction.

Or in another example, perhaps your path includes serving people in your job as the customer service representative for the local telephone company. And one day you decide to quit and travel to Bali, spending 220 hours in training to become an eighth level Yogi instructor. Will your coworkers wonder if you lost your mind? Perhaps... Yet probably not if you let them know you decided to serve others by teaching yoga in retreats instead of sitting at a desk for the phone company. You simply shifted from the second lane to the fourth lane of your path.

A very important part of the concept of change is that you must understand that your partner is changing just as you are.

While you have the same toolbox there can be times when your partner will change and do something a little weird, strange, silly, or outrageous. If you recognize they are merely changing along your path you then understand and can put that into context. For example if you both seem to be in the business fast lane of your mutual path, and then your partner decides to stop and pick wildflowers for two months, you recognize that they are simply changing into the slow lane on that path. Thus, from your fast lane you can appropriately support and care for them in the slow lane.

Conversely, if you don't comprehend they're changing; you become confused, bewildered, and frustrated because they are no longer in the fast lane with you. This then degrades the relationship.....when in reality you're still going to the same place but for the moment just traveling at different speeds.

Returning to our previous example, when you (the hard-charging corporate executive) and your partner (the telephone company customer service operator) suddenly find yourselves following a band and undergoing 220 hours of Yogi training, has your successful relationship spun out of control? Does your partner think you flipped out, and do you wonder what the heck happened to that person you met so long ago?

Just the opposite! This is a great relationship development moment! Since you are on the same path, and have a similar emotional toolkit, you both understand each other are changing. Although initially surprising, you understand the need to change because you're both on the same path and you've had discussions about periodic changes each of you may make. You both decide it would be great to both get yogi training and then follow the band. Then you go back to your new corporate executive project and your partner starts a yoga center, and your relationship grows closer and more rewarding.

This is just one in a long stream of large and small changes you have both made over the years which then serve to further strengthen and enrich your successful relationship.

To summarize, The Unified Theory of Relationship Success states that a successful relationship is always developed when people have an initial physical attraction, they find themselves on the same path, and then they mutually recognize they are continually changing along that path!

Continually applying The Unified Theory of Relationship Success in your life to find your partner will result will result in a lifelong relationship with a solid and health base. From here, the natural byproducts become ever increasing love, caring, honesty, peace, harmony, communication, sex, respect and all other characteristics you and your partner choose to include along your path to a successful relationship.

And Voila!

By applying The Unified Theory
of Relationship Success,
you and your partner are now creating
a very successful lifelong relationship!

www.ingramcontent.com/pod-product-compliance
Lightning Source LLC
Chambersburg PA
CBHW031542040426
42445CB00010B/663